Pompeii
AD 79

A city buried by a volcanic eruption

VIC PARKER

www.raintreepublishers.co.uk
Visit our website to find out more information about **Raintree** books.

To order:
☎ Phone 44 (0) 1865 888113
▤ Send a fax to 44 (0) 1865 314091
▢ Visit the Raintree bookshop at **www.raintreepublishers.co.uk**
to browse our catalogue and order online.

First published in Great Britain by Raintree,
Halley Court, Jordan Hill, Oxford OX2 8EJ, part of
Harcourt Education.

Raintree is a registered trademark of Harcourt
Education Ltd.

© Harcourt Education Ltd 2006
The moral right of the proprietor has been
asserted.

Editorial: Andrew Farrow and Christine Mc Cafferty
Design: Victoria Bevan and AMR Design Ltd
Illustrations: David Woodroffe
Picture Research: Maria Joannou and
   Ginny Stroud-Lewis
Production: Chloe Bloom

Originated by Modern Age
Printed and bound in China by South
   China Printing Company

10 digit ISBN 1 406 20290 8
13 digit ISBN 978 1 4062 0290 8

10 09 08 07 06
10 9 8 7 6 5 4 3 2 1

British Library Cataloguing in Publication Data
Parker, Vic
Pompeii AD 79. - (When disaster struck)
937.7
A full catalogue record for this book is available
from the British Library.

Acknowledgements
The publishers would like to thank the following
for permission to reproduce photographs:
AKG Images 21 (Erich Lessing), 23, 28; Alamy
Images 13 (Ace Stock Limited), 18 (Pam Fraser),
33 (Ace Stock Limited), 39 (Travel-Shots),
45 (Culligen Photos), 46 (Sergio Pitzmitz);
Corbis 4 (Jim Sugar), 6 (Roger Ressmeyer), 10
(Seamus Culligan/ZUMA), 11 (Corbis), 12 (Vinc
Streano), 17 (Werner Forman), 20 (Araldo de
Luca), 26 (Archivo Iconograifco SA), 30 (Michael
S Yamashita), 31 (Jonathan Blair), 32 (Mimo
Jodice), 36 (SYGMA/Jacques Langevin), 40
(/Roger Ressmeyer), 42 (Araldo de Luca), 48
(SYGMA/Harford Chloe), 49 (Jonathan Blair);
Getty Images 44 (Hulton Archive); John Seely
14, 16, 19, 24, 25, 38; The Ancient Art and
Architecture Collection 27; The Art Archive 43
(Bibliotheque des Art Descoratifs Paris/Dagli
Orti); The Bridgeman 'Art Library 35 (Musee de
Petit-Palais, France).

Cover painting of the eruption of Mount Vesuvius,
reproduced with permission of Corbis (Gianni
Dagli Orti).

The publishers would like to thank Dr Damian
Robinson and Dr Barry Hobson, both of the Anglo
American Project in Pompeii, for their assistance
in the preparation of this book.

CONTENTS

Any words appearing in the text in bold, **like this**, are explained in the glossary.

A CITY BURIED BY A VOLCANIC ERUPTION

Pompeii, AD **79**

IN DANGER'S WAY

Imagine being in the path of a volcanic eruption.

There is a mighty rumble. The pavement you are walking on shudders. You are thrown to the ground. You scramble up as a massive black cloud blots out the sky. A shower of burning ash and fiery bits of rock begin pouring down. You cry out in pain and shock.

People around you are screaming and running in all directions. You run too, but the heat melts your shoes and burns your feet. You weave through fires and dodge collapsing buildings. You breathe in burning dust. You choke and gasp, struggling to escape. But where can you escape to?

This is what happened on 24 August AD 79, in the **Roman** town of Pompeii, when Mount Vesuvius **erupted**.

In a volcanic eruption, burning-hot material from deep inside the Earth blasts up above ground.

IN THE
SHADOW OF
VESUVIUS

Pompeii, AD 79

THE TOWN OF POMPEII

In the first century AD, Pompeii was a large, lively Roman town in southern Italy.

The town was home to about 20,000 people. Thousands more visited each year. It lay on a part of the coast called the Bay of Naples. Pompeii was a busy port and an important centre for business. It was probably a holiday resort as well. Many rich people from Rome had splendid houses there with beautiful gardens.

The streets were lined with shops, cafes, and bars. There were several temples, public baths, a **forum**, two theatres, and an **amphitheatre**. This was an arena where Pompeiians watched their favourite sport – warriors called **gladiators** fighting to the death.

Towering above the town was a huge mountain called Vesuvius. Vesuvius was in fact a mighty volcano.

This photograph shows what the town of Pompeii looks like today.

HOW VESUVIUS FORMED

Pompeii lay only about 10 kilometres (6 miles) away from Vesuvius. The town was hundreds of years old, but Vesuvius had been developing for around 17,000 years. It had formed at a weak point (fault line) in the Earth's surface. This line stretches a long way up and down Italy. Vesuvius is just one in a chain of volcanoes that runs along the west coast of Italy and includes the islands off the south west coast.

Deep underground, towards the Earth's centre, hot liquid rock called **magma** flows. Vesuvius began to form when magma started to rise up to the weak point in the surface. The magma was very thick and sticky, like boiling glue. It boiled and bubbled, creating gas that could not escape.

Enormous **pressure** built up underground. Eventually, the gas exploded through the surface, bursting a hole called a **vent**. Then Vesuvius lay quietly for hundreds of years, while the pressure built up again. There was another eruption and hundreds of years later, another. This cycle carried on for thousands of years.

DIFFERENT TYPES OF ERUPTION

Volcanoes do not always explode. If the magma is thin, gas bubbles under the ground can easily escape to the surface. The magma rises through the vent and flows slowly down the sides of the volcano. This happened in 2002 at Europe's largest volcano, Mount Etna in Sicily. Fortunately the deadly river of fire did not reach any towns.

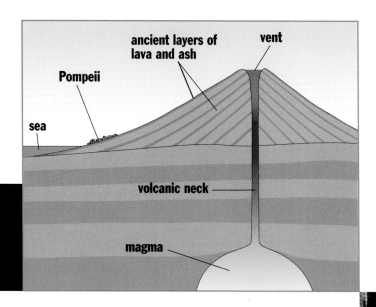

The land Pompeii was built on was actually an ancient lava flow from Vesuvius.

The eruptions at Vesuvius were not always the same. Sometimes, burning rock, ashes, **cinders,** and dust were launched into the air. At other times, the magma itself shot up and out. Each time the material fell back around the vent. Gradually the **lava** layers built up making Vesuvius higher and higher.

Volcanic material is very good for soil because it contains **minerals** that make the soil **fertile**. A few years after every eruption, the grass, plants, and trees grew back fast and strong. The excellent soil attracted people to live on the land around Vesuvius.

By the 4th century BC, many people lived and farmed in the area. The volcano erupted during this period, around 320 BC. A few years later, the Romans invaded the area. They started the towns of Pompeii and Herculaneum. They called the region "Campania Felix", which means "successful countryside". The volcano Vesuvius remained quiet for hundreds of years.

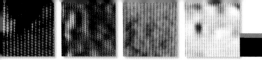

LIVING ON LAVA

By the first century AD, the people of Pompeii did not realize that fire still raged deep inside Vesuvius. To them, it was just a huge, grassy, peaceful mountain.

Modern historians have found writings by a Roman man called Strabo. He was an expert in **geography**. Strabo guessed that Vesuvius had once been a volcano, but he thought that it was no longer **active**. He wrote, "Above these places towers Mount Vesuvius, wholly occupied by beautiful fields all around [...] The summit itself is mainly flat [...] with cracks opening in the rocks, which are sooty on the surface [...] Some may suppose that this place once burned and had craters of fire that later died out [...]"

The Pompeiians were not the only people living in the shadow of Vesuvius. A little further around the bay was the neighbouring town of Herculaneum. Herculaneum was smaller than Pompeii, but it was still a busy, thriving place. It was right on the sea, and the harbour was always packed with fishing boats. It was also a popular holiday spot for people from nearby cities, such as Naples and Rome.

Everywhere in Pompeii you are aware of Mount Vesuvius looming large over the town.

This satellite photo shows the approximate position of Roman towns in the Bay of Naples. Volcanic eruptions have changed the coastline since AD 79.

Pompeii and Herculaneum had long, straight roads that criss-crossed each other. These separated the building areas into blocks. The blocks were divided up into houses, shops, and workshops. Each building connected with the next, so rich and poor people lived closely together. The main streets were always busy with carts and people.

There were several other towns around the Bay of Naples. These included Oplontis, Stabiae, and Misenum. There were also many **villas**, little villages, and large farms on the slopes of Vesuvius itself. There were many busy industries that produced delicious olive oil, wine, a fish sauce called garum, and fine woollen cloth. In the first century AD, the Bay of Naples was one of the most crowded parts of Italy.

VOLCANOES AND PEOPLE

There are people living near active volcanoes all over the world today. In North America, millions live around a chain of volcanoes called the Cascades. The largest active volcanoes include:

- Mount St Helens, Mount Rainier, Mount Baker, and Glacier Peak in Washington State

- Mount Hood, Mount Jefferson, Three Sisters, Newberry, and Crater Lake in Oregon

- Medicine Lake, Mount Shasta, and Lassen Peak in northern California.

A BRUSH WITH DESTRUCTION

On 5 February AD 62, the Bay of Naples was shaken by a violent earthquake. It damaged homes and public buildings all over the area. The towns of Pompeii and Herculaneum were worst affected. Some blocks were entirely ruined. In other blocks, buildings partly crumbled or cracked. Many people were killed and the survivors were terrified. Many of them lost their homes, their possessions, their businesses, or even their family and friends.

No one understood that the earthquake had been caused by pressure rising inside Vesuvius. A thick layer of lava had hardened in the vent over hundreds of years. It acted like a solid plug, blocking up the volcano's mouth (crater). Gases had risen inside Vesuvius, but were not able to escape through the plug. The gases rumbled underground trying to get to the surface. This is what caused a wide area around the volcano to shudder and shake.

Pompeii's forum measured 137 metres (450 feet) by 47 metres (156 feet). It was badly damaged in the earthquake of AD 62. Many statues and columns crumbled to the ground.

The theatre at Pompeii could seat up to 5,000 people.

Pompeii and Herculaneum were so badly damaged that the emperor (ruler) of Rome sent an official to take charge of the situation. Soon grand plans were drawn up to repair the towns. The work was going to take a lot of money and over 20 years to complete.

The rebuilding turned Pompeii and Herculaneum into giant construction sites. The people were determined to make their towns even better than before.

As the people of Pompeii and Herculaneum rebuilt their towns, they thought that they had avoided disaster. They had no idea that they would soon face even greater terror and destruction.

"LAID LOW BY AN EARTHQUAKE"

"Pompeii, the famous city in Campania, has been laid low by an earthquake [...] it caused great destruction [...] part of the town of Herculaneum is in ruins, and even the structures which are left are shaky [...] some people were so shocked that they wandered about as if deprived of their wits [...]"
Seneca, a Roman, writing about the earthquake of AD 62.

THE
DAWN OF
DISASTER

Pompeii, AD 79

IN HONOUR OF VULCAN

Like many other ancient peoples, the Romans thought that volcanoes were caused by the gods.

They believed that a **blacksmith** god called Vulcan worked deep inside the Earth. The Romans thought that the fire from volcanoes were flames from his **forge**.

Vulcan's feast day was 23 August. Every year this was a Roman public holiday. In AD 79, the streets of Pompeii were probably filled with crowds buying snacks and souvenirs from stalls, musicians, jugglers, acrobats, dancers, and fortune-tellers. There would have been plays and sports competitions.

People would have made **offerings** and prayed to Vulcan. No one would have known that there was about to be a massive volcanic eruption.

This mosaic shows street performers acting out a comedy. They often performed on feast days and other holidays.

DISASTER LOOMS

During the celebrations, the people of Pompeii and the surrounding area would have felt a few small earth **tremors**. It was unsettling, but no one panicked. There had been several others over the past week or so. They were gentle and did not cause much damage. Perhaps a few flakes of plaster fell off wall **frescoes** and some fine cracks appeared in **mosaics**.

People did not know that the tremors were caused by underground gas trying to find its way out of Vesuvius. Since the large earthquake of AD 62, enormous pressure had built up inside the volcano.

The local people did not suspect any danger. When night fell on 23 August AD 79, they went to bed as usual.

The rooms in a Roman house were laid out around a courtyard. This courtyard was called an atrium. The atrium had a partly-open roof. Rainwater would fall in and collect in a cistern (water tank) below.

Sometime after midnight, when most people were sleeping soundly, there was a small explosion inside Vesuvius. Some of the gas trapped inside the volcano burst out. It sent a steaming ashy cloud billowing into the black night sky.

Some of the people in Pompeii and Herculaneum must have been woken up by the blast and trembling ground. But they did not know what it was. Most of them would have turned over in their beds and gone back to sleep. A few might have stayed awake, worrying.

A Pompeiian banker called Lucius Caecilius Jucundus had had his household **shrine** decorated with scenes showing the disaster of AD 62. He and his family prayed at it regularly. They probably asked the gods to keep them safe from any more dangers. Maybe Lucius prayed at it now, afraid of the strange noises and tremors in the dark of the night.

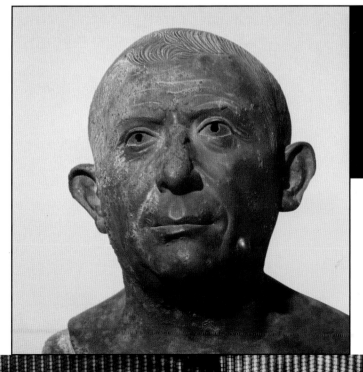

This bronze bust is probably of Lucius Caecilius Jucundus, although it might be of his father. Archaeologists found it in Lucius's house.

THE LAST MORNING IN POMPEII

When day dawned on 24 August AD 79, the workers of Pompeii woke up to business as usual. Shopkeepers hurried to throw open their doors, draw back their shutters, and display their goods. Bar owners moved heavy jars of wine into place to begin selling to customers. Bakers lit fires in ovens. Slaves washed counters and worktops, and swept floors.

This is what one of the main shopping streets in Pompeii, the Via del Vesuvio, looks like today.

The streets were teeming with people, carts, and animals. There was so much traffic every day that the roads were filled with dirt and mud. There were raised stepping stones so people could cross from one pavement to another without getting dirty.

This is a bar that belonged to a man called Asellina. The holes in the marble counter were to hold tall jars that had pointed bases. Many bars sold food, too.

Many Pompeiians headed straight to the forum. This main square was where all the government buildings were. All **official business** was done there. Around the forum were the law courts and the main food market. There were also several temples around the forum. People went to them throughout the week to worship. All these grand buildings were still being repaired after the damage done by the terrible earthquake 17 years before.

As the workers did their early morning **chores**, some might have looked up at Vesuvius looming over the town. White clouds were rising up from the crater into the bright-blue summer sky. No one realized that this was steam from the magma rising inside the volcano.

THE PEOPLE OF POMPEII

Some Pompeiians were free people and some were slaves. Free people owned houses and ran businesses. Slaves did all the manual work for them. Wealthy people often had their names and pictures of themselves carved or painted onto their walls. Poor people often scribbled about themselves on the walls of public places. Someone might have written about a girl he loved, or gladiator he supported. All this writing helps historians find out about the people who lived in Pompeii.

THE HOMES OF THE WEALTHY

In the homes of the wealthy, the morning of 24 August 79 AD started just like any other. Rich men got up early because poorer people always came to visit them. These visitors were called clients. The rich man was their patron. The clients waited and took turns to see their patron, to ask for his help in business and other matters. Some rich men had so many clients to see that they were kept busy all morning! They looked forward to the afternoon, when they would relax at the public baths with their friends.

Wealthy women got up and dressed at a relaxed pace. They spent half the morning being pampered by slaves. They took a long time putting on heavy make-up and doing their hair. Then they carefully chose their clothes and jewellery. Finally they were ready to start the day.

This is a wealthy couple from Pompeii. They are believed to be Terentius Neo and his wife.

The gardens at the House of the Vettii are still beautiful today.

The rich Vettii family had a magnificent home. In their house, as in wealthy houses all over Pompeii, the kitchen staff prepared lunch. Pompeiians loved good food! The Vettii family's cook had several pots and pans simmering away over the kitchen fire.

Lunch was going to be in a beautiful dining room, decorated with wall paintings of **cherubs**, that opened onto the garden. It was next to magnificent gardens where water splashed down the fountains. Marble statues decorated the elegant walkways. Slaves hurried to prepare the couches where the family would lie to eat.

Maybe on this particular morning there was no birdsong in the gardens. Birds and animals often sense when an earthquake or eruption is going to happen. They become distressed and often run away from the area. Birds may have vanished from gardens all over Pompeii. Dogs may have been whining. If so, people must have been very puzzled.

THE BEGINNING OF THE END

Pompeii, AD **79**

VESUVIUS ERUPTS

At about 1:00 p.m. a mighty roar suddenly filled the air, the ground shook violently, and everyone screamed in terror.

People rushed into the streets to find out what was going on. Those who saw Vesuvius cried out in alarm. A huge, smoky cloud was spurting high into the air from the mountain. Vesuvius was erupting!

The lava plug inside the crater was blown to bits by escaping gas. Then the volcano threw out enormous quantities of red-hot ash. **Pumice** rock also rained down. The material that flew out of the volcano every second weighed about as much as 300 large trucks. It hurled kilometres high into the sky, faster than a jet plane. The scorching pieces began raining down on the people of Pompeii. They ran for cover.

This painting shows people struggling to escape from the erupting volcano.

SITTING OUT THE STORM

The citizens of Pompeii sheltered wherever they could. They waited for the strange storm to pass. To their horror, it did not. After 90 minutes, the dark cloud from Vesuvius had spread across the entire sky. It was as dark as nightfall. People had to light their lamps to see. The burning rocks continued raining from the sky. Soon they lay knee high on the streets and rooftops.

Some of the falling pieces were as big as apples. These crashed right through the roof tiles. All the time, earth tremors shook the buildings, toppling furniture and sending things smashing to the floor. People everywhere panicked. They did not know whether to stay where they were or try to escape from the town.

This photograph shows a large washing vat at Stephanus's laundry. An important part of the business was cleaning and dyeing new cloth.

This is what Pompeii's palaestrum looks like today. The rectangle on the right was a swimming pool. Like a modern pool, it had a shallow end and a deep end.

At Stephanus's laundry in the town centre, people locked and barred the wide entrance door. They hid behind it. As the hours passed, the pumice piled up higher and higher outside. They huddled together in fear, praying to the gods.

Many young men were exercising at the large open-air sports ground called the palaestrum. They were in training to join the Roman army.

The young men sheltered in a room there. They had been preparing for the terrors of battle. However, this was worse than anything they had imagined. The ground was heaving. The walls were cracking. The roof was crumbling.

"BLOTCHED AND DIRTY"

People from far across the bay saw the towering eruption cloud. A man known as Pliny the Younger watched it from the town of Misenum. This is how he described it:

" [...] it rose to a great height on a sort of trunk and then split off into branches [...] In places it looked white, elsewhere blotched and dirty, according to the amount of soil and ashes it carried with it [...]"

ABANDONED BY THE GODS

**VOLCANIC ACTIVITY
ON 24 AUGUST AD 79**

1:00 p.m. Vesuvius erupts, spitting out 10,000 tonnes (11,020 US tons) of material every second.

2:30 p.m. The volcano's column reaches 16 kilometres (10 miles) high. This is higher than jets fly.

By 5:30 p.m. Vesuvius ejects 40,000 tonnes (44,100 US tons) of material every second. The column rises to 27 kilometres (16.8 miles).

By 7:30 p.m. Vesuvius ejects nearly 100,000 tonnes (110,200 US tons) of material every second. The volcano's column reaches 30 kilometres (18.6 miles). This is nearly three and a half times as high as Mount Everest.

Thousands of Pompeiians decided that their best chance of survival was to leave the town. Modestus, the baker, probably was one of them. He left 81 loaves to burn inside his oven and then it seems, he fled. Crowds of terrified people made for the town gates. They struggled to walk on the layers of pumice. They cried in fear, pain, and desperation. Flaming fragments pelted them from the skies. Roofs and buildings came crashing down around them.

In the Temple of Isis, the priests also decided to run away. They had no idea if it was safer outside the town, in the countryside. But they realized that if they stayed where they were they would probably die. The priests hurriedly gathered together some of their temple treasures such as money and gold.

At Modestus's bakery today, you can still see the huge oven and the tall mills used for grinding corn into flour. Large mills were turned by donkeys walking round and round. Small mills were turned by slaves.

As they staggered through the streets, a priest was hit by falling pumice. He collapsed and died at the corner of a main street called the Via dell'Abbondanza. The survivors fled to a meeting place called the Triangular Forum. The building began to crumble and they ran again, dropping their treasures.

A couple more were killed, but one took shelter in a nearby house. However, he was not safe for long. A nearby building collapsed and rubble heaped up outside the front door. He was trapped! He found an axe. He began trying to chop his way through the thick wall to the house next door. He did not make it.

This wall painting shows priests at the Temple of Isis carrying out a ceremony. Every afternoon, they blessed water, the source of all life.

DEATH AND DESTRUCTION

Pompeii, AD 79

WIDESPREAD PANIC

The wind was blowing away from the town of Herculaneum, so no ash fell there. Still there was panic and fear.

The people were horrified by the cloud coming up from Vesuvius, blacking out the sky. Earth tremors shook buildings. Plaster fell off walls. Roofs caved in.

It seemed that the only escape was across the sea. Some people might have gone by boat, but over 200 were left on the beach. They waited anxiously, hoping that people from elsewhere around the bay would rescue them.

Boats did set out from other places. But most could not get through the pumice and ash raining down over the sea. Pliny the Elder was an **admiral** in the Roman **navy** at Misenum. He sailed to help a friend, but was forced to turn away. His ship was blown along the coast and he took shelter at a house in Stabiae.

The people of Herculaneum saw lightning in the eruption cloud from Vesuvius. This painting shows the flashes of lightning that often appear in volcano eruption clouds. Scientists are not sure why this happens.

DISASTER AT HERCULANEUM

As night fell, Vesuvius was hurling out burning rock and ash ever faster. By about 1:00 a.m., the early hours of the next morning, the volcano's vent could no longer stand up under the immense pressure. It collapsed, making the vent even wider. Material now shot up into the air at an incredible rate of 150,000 tonnes (165,300 US tons) per second.

A dark cloud towered about 33 kilometres (20.5 miles) above the vent. Suddenly the cloud collapsed. A glowing cloud of red-hot gas, ash, and rock fragments rushed down the sides of Vesuvius. The temperature of this material was around 815°C (1500°F). That is four times hotter than the oven in your kitchen.

It raced straight towards Herculaneum and reached the town in only 4 minutes. The only people still there were the very sick or old. Meanwhile, hundreds of people were still waiting on the beach hoping to be rescued. The cloud was so fast that no one even saw or felt it coming. They were all killed instantly by the heat and ash.

A pyroclastic flow° destroys everything in its path.

Archaeologists have found skletons on the beach at Herculaneum. Some of the bones were burned black by the intense heat.

Just minutes later, another massive cloud engulfed the town. This one was full of heavier chunks of pumice and rock. It also swept along fallen material, such as wooden beams and roof tiles and bricks, in a huge landslide. All this material fell on to Herculaneum. It began to bury the buildings.

The same thing happened at Oplontis. A short while later, a second mass hit the towns.

PYROCLASTIC FLOWS

Modern scientists have studied clouds of material from volcanoes that race along close to the ground. They have discovered that the fastest ones can travel at around 720 kilometres (450 miles) per hour. Scientists call these clouds of material pyroclastic flows, or sometimes *nuées ardents* (this is French for "glowing clouds").

CATASTROPHE AT POMPEII

PYROCLASTIC FLOWS ON 25 AUGUST AD 79

1:00–2:00 a.m. Glowing clouds of material engulf Herculaneum, Oplontis, and the nearby area.

6:30 a.m. A cloud of poisonous gas rushes into Pompeii.

7:30–7:45 a.m. Two bigger, hotter floods of ash blast into Pompeii.

8:00 a.m. Another even bigger surge overcomes Pompeii. It reaches many kilometres beyond the town, across the Bay of Naples.

Meanwhile most of the residents of Pompeii managed to flee from the town. However, well over 2,000 people remained there. Some thought it safer to stay than to go out in the fiery storm. Many were too terrified to set off into unknown danger. Others were too old or sick to leave.

At dawn the sky stayed dark, full of the ash cloud from Vesuvius. The horrified townspeople must have thought the Sun had not risen. It must have seemed like the world was ending.

More desperate people decided to leave. But the ash and pumice had piled up in front of their doors and windows around 3 metres (nearly 10 feet) high. Many people were trapped indoors like Julius Polybius, a wealthy merchant and important citizen. He was sheltering in two back rooms of his house with his wife, his pregnant daughter and her husband, and several other members of his household. Other people managed somehow to push their way outside. In the house of Marcus Lucretius, some men, women, and children made it out into the garden.

The house of Marcus Lucretius can still be seen today.

But time had run out for the people of Pompeii. At about 6:30 p.m. there was a tremendous rumble and then a wave of blistering heat. A flood of poisonous gases from Vesuvius swamped the town. Any people and animals outside choked and suffocated. An hour later, two even hotter rushes of ash blasted the buildings. For those indoors, it was as if they were breathing fire. Anyone still alive collapsed to the ground and died in agony.

These plaster models (see p. 44) were made of the people who died near one of the gates of Pompeii.

PANIC IN THE COUNTRYSIDE

All this time, the thousands of people who had fled from Pompeii were stumbling across the countryside in every direction. They struggled to breathe because the air was heavy with red-hot dust. Burning ash and pumice continued to rain down on them.

Many people were knocked to the ground, dead or injured. Often their family and friends were forced to leave them behind. They had to keep going if they wanted to survive. They had no idea where the cloud from Vesuvius ended – if it ended at all. They just knew they had to run as fast as they could.

At about 8:00 a.m. the biggest ash cloud yet surged from Mount Vesuvius. It raced up behind the people fleeing from Pompeii. Many felt its heat and turned round. They were horrified to see dense smoke rushing towards them, glowing with fire. It washed over them. Suddenly, their skin was scorching and they were choking in poisonous fumes. It was impossible to outrun it. Thousands of people died.

The ash surge was so enormous it spread right across the Bay of Naples. The glowing cloud billowed towards towns and villages in both the north and south of the bay. It turned the skies black as it approached. People found themselves breathing its burning gases.

In the town of Stabiae, Pliny the Elder tried to stand up to run away. It was so difficult to breathe that two slaves had to help him out of his chair. He was overcome by the fumes and collapsed to the ground, where he suffocated. Many other people staggered in the darkness through the smoky, hot air to try to get away.

The edge of the enormous surge reached Pliny the Younger in Misenum. This was about 32 kilometres (20 miles) away from Mount Vesuvius. He later wrote about it in a letter. Pliny said that the thick, smoky cloud covered the sea and spread over the land like a flood. He ran from it with his mother. The light was so dim that they could hardly see where they were going. The roads were crowded, so Pliny and his mother tried to escape into some fields.

As they ran, ashes blew over them from behind. Then there was total darkness. All around them, women were crying, children were wailing, and men were shouting. Pliny turned to see a strange glow approaching. First he thought that it was daylight, but then he realized it was fire! Pliny believed that everyone would die. But he lived to tell the tale.

This artwork is called *The Last Days of Pompeii*. It was painted in the 1800s.

AFTER THE DISASTER

Pompeii, AD 79

THE ERUPTION ENDS

Mount Vesuvius had finally thrown out its last flood of red-hot ash.

Enormous amounts of steam had spurted into the air during the eruption. Now, this turned into boiling rain! The scorching water poured down and mixed with the tonnes of ash and rock that had fallen. It turned into rivers of mud that flooded down Vesuvius in the direction of Herculaneum.

It was more than a day before the skies cleared and sunlight returned. The whole southern end of the Bay of Naples looked like a desert of grey ash. Where Pompeii had stood, only the tips of the tallest buildings were still visible. Several other towns, including Herculaneum, had totally disappeared.

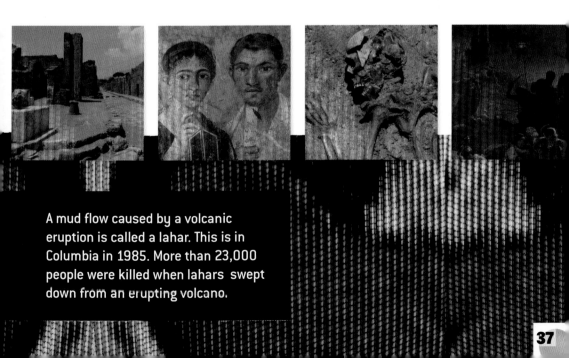

A mud flow caused by a volcanic eruption is called a lahar. This is in Columbia in 1985. More than 23,000 people were killed when lahars swept down from an erupting volcano.

DEALING WITH THE DESTRUCTION

THE SCALE OF THE ERUPTION

In all Vesuvius rocketed out more than 9 billion tonnes (nearly 10 billion US tons) of volcanic material. Ash fell as far away as Egypt and North Africa. Pompeii was covered by volcanic material 4 metres (13 feet) deep. Herculaneum was covered by volcanic material and mud 25 metres (82 feet) deep.

Many of those who survived the eruption were separated from their family and friends. Now they hunted desperately for their loved ones. People hurried back to the buried area to search for anyone who might still be alive underground. It was a wilderness of grey ash. It was very difficult to know where to dig.

The Roman army formed rescue parties, but it was hopeless. No one could have survived being buried like that. The gangs had to dig deep shafts to reach anything. They were forced to give up looking for people. They were able to rescue just a few important treasures instead, such as some statues from Pompeii's forum.

There were many statues of emperors, gods, and goddesses around Pompeii's forum. This statue was close by, at the temple of Apollo. It shows the god, Apollo, as an archer, although today his bow and arrow are missing.

The Roman emperor put some top officials in charge of the disaster zone. Their most urgent job was to provide emergency aid. Thousands of people had been left with nothing but the clothes they were wearing. Hundreds of homeless, penniless families flooded into the big cities of Naples and Sorrento looking for help. The officials said that any houses, land, or possessions belonging to people who had died should be sold. The money had to be given to the homeless.

Eventually trees and grass covered the towns buried by the eruption of Vesuvius.

They planned to dig the towns out and rebuild them so that everyone could return to their homes and jobs. They soon realized that this was an impossible task. All the buried places had to be abandoned.

Seasons came and went, and the land over the towns remained undisturbed. Grass, plants, and trees grew until the area became part of the countryside once more. People built new houses, villas, and villages around the area. Centuries passed with no sign that Pompeii and Herculaneum had ever existed.

THE LOST CITIES ARE DISCOVERED

Pompeii, AD 79

ANCIENT FINDS

In 1594 workers were digging a water channel near Vesuvius when they uncovered some painted walls.

But nobody took much notice. At that time people were not interested in **archaeology** and the ancient world.

In 1689 workmen unearthed a stone with "POMPEIA" carved into it. People thought it was the name of an ancient person. Again, nobody paid much attention.

In 1706, workers digging a well further up the coast found decorated walls. The land was now owned by an Austrian prince. He ordered them to dig tunnels to find out what was there. They discovered it was Roman ruins. Over the next seven years, they removed many precious marble statues and bronze ornaments.

In 1738, a Spaniard called Rocco de Alcubierre continued to hunt for more treasures. He realized that one colourful wall belonged to the theatre of Herculaneum.

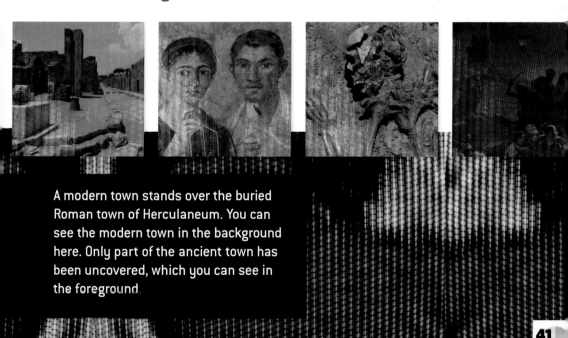

A modern town stands over the buried Roman town of Herculaneum. You can see the modern town in the background here. Only part of the ancient town has been uncovered, which you can see in the foreground.

POMPEII IS DISCOVERED

The King of Naples ordered Alcubierre to keep digging tunnels to explore Herculaneum. Alcubierre stayed for years, and found all sorts of valuable Roman objects.

A Swiss man called Karl Weber helped him. Weber was more interested in the wonderful buildings than in the treasures. The mud and volcanic material had kept them in very good condition. Weber worked hard to explore the town without causing damage.

In 1748 workers found the buried ruins of more houses, not far from Herculaneum. The King of Naples ordered Alcubierre to start digging there, too. It became clear that this was the town of Pompeii. The ground was softer than at Herculaneum, and so it was easier to dig. In 1765, work had to stop at Herculaneum because the tunnels filled with an unsafe gas. From then on, they mainly worked at Pompeii.

▶ "POMPEII SUPRISES EVERYONE"

"Pompeii surprises everyone by its **compactness** and its smallness of scale [...] The streets are narrow [...] the houses small [...] even the public buildings, the **bench tomb** at the town gate, the temple and a villa hereby look more like **architectural models** or dolls' houses than real buildings. But their rooms, passages and arcades are gaily painted [...]"

Johann Wolfgang von Goethe was a German writer who visited Pompeii in 1787.

A **mosaic** showing Alexander the Great in battle was found in 1831, in a home in Pompeii. Alexander the Great, as head of an united Greek army, conquered much of Asia after 336 B.C.

This painting shows Pompeii as it would have looked to visitors in the 1700s.

In the years that followed, Italian, Spanish, and French rulers were very interested in investigating Pompeii. When Weber and Alcubierre stopped, the rulers appointed other experts to keep the work going. Sometimes prisoners were made to do the actual digging, chained together in pairs.

A small theatre, the Temple of Isis, and the gladiators' **barracks** were uncovered. Skeletons in a villa belonging to a man called Diomedes were found. They lay hugging each other, just as the terrified people had died. A huge, stunning mosaic, showing Alexander the Great in battle, was also uncovered.

By the end of the 1700s, news of Pompeii spread all over the world. Many people travelled to the site to see it for themselves. During the 1800s, there were many important visitors. Among them were Queen Victoria of Britain, Prince Ludwig of Bavaria, English writer Charles Dickens, and American author Mark Twain.

TIMELINE

1594 Workers dig up ruins at the foot of Vesuvius.

1689 Workmen in the same area discover a stone carved with the word "POMPEIA". They do not know what it means.

1706 Workers further around the coast find the buried Roman walls. People start digging there for ancient treasures.

1738 Rocco de Alcubierre realizes that where the treasure hunters are digging is Herculaneum.

1748 Workers find more buried houses near the foot of Vesuvius. People at last realize they have found Pompeii.

BRINGING THE TOWNS BACK TO LIFE

In December 1860 the King of Italy appointed a man called Giuseppe Fiorelli to take charge of Pompeii. Fiorelli drew a plan of the town and divided it into big regions and smaller zones. He numbered all the buildings and wrote careful records of the findings. From then on everyone did the same.

Fiorelli had another brilliant idea. The diggers were finding many skeletons. But they were finding many more body-shaped holes. These were where the ash and rock had hardened around dead people and animals, but the bodies had crumbled away to nothing. Fiorelli thought of using the holes like moulds. He forced a special liquid plaster inside them. When the plaster hardened, it left perfect models of the missing bodies. The models showed incredible details, such as the expressions on people's faces and even the texture of their clothes. The method worked for furniture and objects, too.

Workers excavating (digging up) Pompeii in the 1920s.

Work continues at both sites to this day. Now you can walk all around both towns. You can go in and out of buildings and gardens. They are almost the same as they were in AD 79. You can get an excellent idea of what it was like to live in Pompeii and Herculaneum.

There is still more to be dug up. Some universities have projects at the sites. Young people can take part in organized archaeological digs.

Today Pompeii is one of Italy's most-visited ancient sites.

COULD IT HAPPEN AGAIN?

Pompeii, AD 79

VESUVIUS REMAINS ACTIVE

After Vesuvius erupted in AD 79, red-hot magma still bubbled underneath, deep inside the Earth.

Over the centuries, the volcano has erupted again from time to time, but on a much smaller scale. Sometimes there were ash clouds and sometimes lava flows.

In 1631 there was an eruption almost as violent as the one that buried Pompeii and Herculaneum. It caused terrible earthquakes and a tidal wave. Thousands of people died in burning ash from the volcano. Since then there have been many smaller eruptions. A second vent has formed on the south side of the volcano.

In 1841 scientists set up the Vesuvius **Observatory** to watch the volcano around the clock. There was a slow lava flow in 1944. They are waiting for the next eruption.

Today millions of people live in the Bay of Naples area and thousands of tourists visit each year. It is one of the world's most crowded volcanic regions.

WATCHING AND WAITING

Today there are about 1,500 active volcanoes around the world. Scientists have built volcano-watching stations like the Vesuvius Observatory in many risk areas. They keep a record of any changes in volcanoes and their surroundings. They look for things like cracks forming in the ground, plants withering for no apparent reason, and changes in the colour of the soil.

They use **hi-tech** equipment to carefully measure the temperature of the ground. They also measure blasts of steam and tiny tremors, and **analyse** the air for gases. This helps them know if an eruption is on its way, and what type and size it might be. If they feel the signs are serious, they warn local people and emergency services.

Before scientists started monitoring volcanoes, there were other terrible disasters similar to Pompeii in AD 79. In 1815 an eruption in Tambora, Indonesia, killed around 10,000 people. Over 80,000 more died from disease and starvation after the eruption.

Today scientists are usually able to give warnings. People can then leave an area before eruptions take place. In the late summer of 1997, residents of the Caribbean island of Montserrat were told to leave. On 26 December, the island's volcano exploded violently. The scientists' warning saved thousands of people.

However, no scientist can predict exactly when an eruption will happen. In early April 1980, scientists in Washington State, United States, warned that Mount St Helens was going to erupt. People were cleared from their homes and were not allowed to go back. A month passed with no eruption. The people who had been moved away grew very frustrated.

The eruption on the island of Montserrat in 1997 was caused by the Soufrière Hills Volcano. Around 11,000 people lived on the island.

On 15 May the police went with them back to their homes for a few hours so that they could collect their belongings. Another trip was planned for 10:00 a.m. the next day. But the volcano erupted 90 minutes before! A scientist taking measurements near the crater was taken by surprise and killed. Another 50 people also died. They had disobeyed instructions and were close to the volcano.

There are many volcanoes that threaten the Bay of Naples today, besides Vesuvius. There are several craters in an area called the Campi Flegri. There is also a volcanic island called Ischia just off the same coast. Officials have drawn up emergency plans in case scientists warn of a big eruption. However, experts disagree on the best way to evacuate the millions of people. Some scientists worry that they might not be able to give enough warning for everyone to get away in time.

Will there be another disaster like that of AD 79? Only time will tell.

VOLCANO FACTS

- Only 20 to 30 volcanoes on Earth erupt every year.

- More than half of the world's active volcanoes encircle the Pacific Ocean in an area known as the "Ring of Fire".

- The world's largest active volcano is Mauna Loa on the island of Hawaii. It is taller than Mount Everest, although most of it is under the sea.

- There are hundreds of active volcanoes under the sea.

- There are volcanoes on other planets, such as Mars, and on the Moon.

TIMELINE

15,000 BC Mount Vesuvius begins to form, erupting many times over the next thousands of years.

c. 700 BC A tribe called the Oscans founds settlements at Pompeii and Herculaneum.

c. 600 BC The ancient Greeks settle in the area.

c. 420 BC A tribe called the Samnites conquer the ancient Greek settlements.

320 BC Mount Vesuvius erupts again. Soon after, the ancient Romans invade the area and people begin to develop the towns. Pompeii is independent, but allied to Rome.

80 BC Pompeii becomes a Roman colony. Seven years later escaped Roman gladiator, Spartacus, hides out on Vesuvius with 70 other gladiators and hundreds of runaway slaves.

c. AD 10 The Roman geographer, Strabo, writes that Vesuvius is no longer an active volcano.

5 Feb AD 62 A violent earthquake caused by pressure rising in Vesuvius shakes the Bay of Naples area. It causes much destruction in the towns of Pompeii and Herculaneum, killing many people.

24 Aug AD 79 Vesuvius erupts violently, totally destroying Pompeii, Herculaneum, Oplontis, and other towns in the Bay of Naples area, killing thousands of people.

AD 203 to 1138 Several small eruptions of Vesuvius – sometimes throwing out ash, sometimes lava.

AD 1594 Workmen digging near Vesuvius uncover painted walls.

AD 1631 Vesuvius erupts almost as violently as in AD 79, causing earthquakes and a tidal wave. Again thousands of people die.

AD 1660 Small, black, cross-shaped pieces of volcanic material rain down from Vesuvius on surrounding villages. The people think it is the work of a local saint.

1689	Workmen digging in the same area as during the 1594 discovery, find a stone with "POMPEIA" carved into it.
1706	Workmen digging further up the coast unearth more decorated walls. Prince d'Elbeuf orders more tunnels to be dug. Over seven years, he finds and removes many Roman treasures.
From 1707	Vesuvius erupts many times over the centuries that follow.
1738	A Spanish treasure-hunter, Rocco de Alcubierre, is working in the tunnels when it becomes clear that the ruins are the town of Herculaneum. The King of Naples orders work to continue.
1748	Workers find more buried ruins some kilometres away and the King of Naples orders Alcubierre to begin digging there, too. It becomes clear that this is the town of Pompeii.
1765	Work stops at Herculaneum because of unsafe gas in the tunnels.
1841	Scientists establish an observatory to watch for volcanic activity in Vesuvius.
1860 to 1875	Giuseppe Fiorelli leads the digging at Pompeii.
1924	Amedeo Maiuri begins to lead the digging at Pompeii, uncovering some of the grandest houses.
1927	Amedeo Maiuri starts work again at Herculaneum to uncover the town.
1944	The most recent eruption of Vesuvius. This is a slow lava flow.
1980	Excavations at Pompeii are damaged by an earthquake in the area.

GLOSSARY

active volcano currently erupting or showing signs of activity, such as earthquakes or tremors in the region or release of gases

admiral highest ranking officer in a navy

amphitheatre in ancient Roman times, an oval, sometimes circular, arena for gladiator fights, animal fighting, and chariot racing

analyse study something carefully to find out what it is made up of

archaeology scientific study of the past using very old buildings and objects that have been carefully dug up or uncovered

architectural models smaller sized models of buildings that are planned to be built

barracks a large building where soldiers live

bench tomb big box-like grave, built the right height and size for sitting on

blacksmith someone who makes or fixes things made from iron

cherub angel, but usually depicted as a sweet, chubby child with wings

chore boring job that usually has to be done regularly

cinders pieces of black material that are left over after something has burned

compactness smallness and neatness

erupt when a volcano erupts, red-hot material spouts from its cone and spreads over the surrounding area

fertile good for growing plants in

forge furnace where a blacksmith melts metal to work it

forum large open space in a Roman town. It was the social and business centre of the town and often had important buildings and temples around it.

fresco picture painted on a wall while the plaster is still wet

geography study of the Earth's landscape and weather

gladiator slave or prisoner-of-war who was specially trained to fight to the death. This was a Roman sport.

hi-tech using a lot of technology, such as scientific electronic and digital devices

lava what magma is called when it reaches the surface

magma hot melted rock under the Earth's surface, and in volcanoes

minerals non-living elements or substances found in the ground, such as iron or zinc, that are essential to the nutrition of humans, animals, and plants

mosaic tiny, coloured pieces of stone or tiles, arranged and glued into pictures on walls or floors

navy a country's ships and sailors used in war

observatory building specially designed for watching the surroundings, such as the landscape, weather, or sky

offerings animals that are killed, food, flowers, or precious things that people give to their gods

official business things done or given out by people in power (the government)

pressure force on or against a surface by something pressing on it

pumice light, holey rock from dried volcanic lava

Romans people who ruled a powerful empire over 2,000 years ago. The capital was Rome, Italy. It stretched across most of western Europe, the Middle East, and the north coast of Africa.

shrine display shelf, small building, or other place, especially for worshiping a god or saint

tremor trembling or shuddering movement

vent mouth of a volcano through which volcanic materials come out

villa grand, luxurious country house

FINDING OUT MORE

BOOKS

Awesome Forces of Nature: Violent Volcanoes, Louise and Richard Spilsbury (Heinemann Library, 2005)

Excavating the Past: Ancient Rome, Fiona Macdonald (Heinemann Library, 2004)

Roman Mysteries: The Secrets of Vesuvius and *The Pirates of Pompeii,* Caroline Lawrence (Orion Children's Books, 2002). These books are gripping fiction thrillers set in Pompeii.

Turbulent Planet: Earth Erupts: Volcanoes, Mary Colson (Raintree, 2005)

VOLCANOES ONLINE

www.harcourtschool.com/activity/pompeii
Explore the ancient city of Pompeii and see Vesuvius erupt.

www.pompeiisites.org
The official sites of the excavations of Pompeii, Herculaneum, and Oplontis.

www.bbc.co.uk/history/programmes/pompeii
Trace the final hours of Pompeii. You can also play a game in which you become a Roman detective.

volcano.und.nodak.edu
The 'Volcano World' site tells you everything you want to know about volcanoes around the globe.

www.brookes.ac.uk/geology/8361/2000/angela/home
A trip to Vesuvius by a student from Brookes University in Oxford, UK.

www.archaeology.org/interactive/pompeii
See how the Anglo-American Project in Pompeii is training future archaeologists by giving them the chance to take part in digs in Pompeii. An interesting way to spend the summer.

FURTHER RESEARCH

If you are interested in finding out more about Pompeii, archaeology, or volcanoes, try researching the following topics:

- how volcanoes are formed and why they erupt
- volcanoes that are currently active
- being part of an archaeological dig
- lives, beliefs, and culture of the ancient Romans.

INDEX

Titles in the *When Disaster Struck* series include:

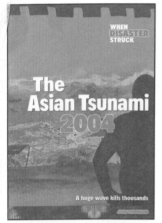

Hardback   1 406 20291 6

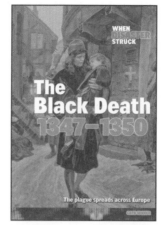

Hardback   1 406 20286 X

Hardback   1 406 20287 8

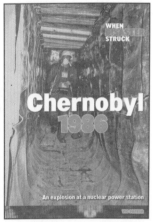

Hardback   1 406 20285 1

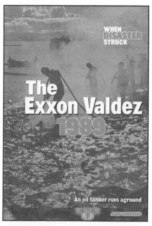

Hardback   1 406 20292 4

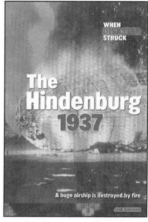

Hardback   1 406 20293 2

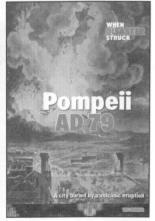

Hardback   1 406 20290 8

Hardback   1 406 20288 6

Find out about other titles from Raintree on our website www.raintreepublishers.co.uk